Raspberry Pi 2

By Solis Tech

Raspberry Pi 2 Programming Made Easy

2nd Edition

Raspberry (2nd Edition) : Raspberry Pi2 Programming Made Easy

Table of Contents

Introduction

Greetings. Thank you for purchasing this book Raspberry Pi 2: Raspberry Pi 2 Programming Made Easy. If you're reading this book then most likely you are here to learn about his nifty new little computer called the Raspberry Pi. In this book, we'll teach you everything that you need to know to get up and running with this little, but powerful computer.

We'll teach you about its parts, its specifications, setting up the operating system, its capabilities and limitations, and ultimately how to do basic programming. We'll discuss the best programming language that works best with the Raspberry Pi and create your first program with it. Without further ado, let's start your Raspberry Pi journey.

Chapter 1: Raspberry Pi – The Basics

What is a Raspberry Pi?

So what is it exactly? We'll it's a small credit-card sized single board computer that is intended to help people learn more about programming, how the computer works, etc. The CPU or Central Processing Unit is basically a system-on-a-chip. What that means is it pairs an ARM processor that is used by a lot of embedded systems and cellular phones with a Broadcom GPU (Graphics Processing Unit), which is a fairly powerful graphics processor that's capable of displaying full resolution 1080p HD video.

The amount of RAM (Random Access Memory) that the Raspberry Pi 2 has is 1 Gigabyte. Its previous iteration, the Raspberry Pi 1 Model A+ and Raspberry Pi 1 Model B has 256MB and 512MB RAM respectively. The RAM is shared by both the CPU and the GPU.

The Raspberry Pi 2 starts at $39.00 and that includes just the board. On the board there are 4 USB ports, 40 General Purpose Input/Output (GPIO) pins, a full 1080p HDMI port, a Network/Ethernet port, a 3.5mm audio and composite video jack, a Raspberry Pi (CSI) Camera interface, a Video (DSI) Display interface, a Micro SD card slot, and a VideoCore 3D graphics core. The GPIO is basically for more advanced users who are going to be adding Arduino accessory boards, ribbon cables for communication with other hardware devices, and major electronics projects; robotics, sensors, etc.

Why Is it Cool to Have a Raspberry Pi?

Most people think the Raspberry Pi is cool because it's a fairly complete computer, it runs on very little power, it's small, and it will not burn a hole through your wallet; it's $39.00, which is less than the cost that you would pay for a dinner with a friend or a loved one. The Raspberry Pi also helps people that are new to computer hardware get into it and get their hands dirty without the cost and risk associated with more expensive standard hardware.

Another thing that's cool about it is that the Graphics Processing Unit is pretty powerful. It can play 1080p HD video, which makes it really attractive to a lot of people as a Media Center PC. In fact, most people buy the Raspberry Pi 2 for that specific reason because it is a cheap multimedia PC.

What Can You Do With a Raspberry Pi?

So what can you do with this thing? Well, just like what was previously mentioned, if you're really new to computer hardware, the Pi can help you learn about those individual components of most modern computers. And if you want to learn how to do programming, the Raspbian operating system that comes with the Raspberry Pi 2 comes with a lot of tools for programming to help you get started.

So you might be asking, why wouldn't you start learning how to program with the computer that you already have? Well, you can. And that's perfectly fine. However, you can think of the Raspberry Pi as your little playground and your test computer that you don't have to worry about breaking if you screw something up. Even if you do break it, you'll only be losing $39.00.

But if you don't care about all that and you don't care about programming or about learning the hardware and so forth, the Raspberry Pi 2 also makes a really great little Media PC. You can get a small case for it, hook it up to the network, install another operating system that's based on Linux called OpenELEC, which is basically a back-end for XBMC (Xbox Media Center), plug it into your TV, and you're ready to start streaming video and audio content on your high-definition TV.

Chapter 2: Hardware Accessories

In this chapter, we're going to talk about some of the hardware and accessories that you're going to need to get started with the Raspberry Pi 2. First, let's start out with the bare necessities. The two things that you'll definitely need are power and an SD card.

Power Requirement

Let's take a moment here and talk about power because it's important. The Raspberry Pi is a little picky about its power source. Learning about what you need here for power could save you a lot of headache later down the road. The Raspberry Pi needs 5 volts. That should be anywhere between 4.75 volts minimum and a maximum of 5.25 volts. It should be at least 700 mAh, but the recommended is 1000 mAh.

The reason for the 1000 mAh recommended power is because when you start plugging in a keyboard, mouse, network cable, and other peripherals, these all pull power away from the system. This is also why some Raspberry Pi 2 users say that 1500 mAh to 2000 mAh is even better. Of course, if you're only doing projects close to your desktop computer and you don't really plan to run the Raspberry Pi 24/7, you could just run it off of your desktop system's power with just a USB cable if you want.

SD Card Storage

There is not on-board storage on the Raspberry Pi. So you need an SD card to run the operating system from and also to store any files. Get at least the Class 4 SD storage. It is recommended that you get the Class 6 or Class 10 if you don't mind spending a little bit more.

However, if it's not available, just get the best one that you can. The cost difference honestly isn't that much, and SD cards are getting cheaper all the time. You'll also need a card reader to transfer the operating system image that you're going to download off of Raspberry Pi's website from your desktop computer to the SD card. You can also buy SD cards with the operating system pre-installed from whosoever your Raspberry Pi vendor is if ever you want to skip the operating system installation on the Pi.

If you want to try out multiple operating systems, you can do that with a single card. However, just keep in mind that you'll overwrite any of your settings that you've played around with in the operating system.

Interacting With the Raspberry Pi

You'll need to decide on how you want to interact with your Raspberry Pi. You can either do it headless over a network, with a keyboard, mouse and monitor, or you can do a combination of both. For network access, you're going to need a network cable; either a CAT5e or CAT6 to connect to your router. There's also a USB WiFi option, which allows you to connect to your router wirelessly.

If you're going headless, you don't really need a USB keyboard and mouse. They are both optional. It just depends on what you want to use the Raspberry Pi for. Just like what was previously mentioned, if you don't want to use the desktop interface, you can skip using a mouse and just plug in a keyboard. If you're using it as a media center and navigate XBMC, a wireless Bluetooth keyboard is a fantastic option if you want to sit on your couch and navigate your media center.

If you're only planning to login remotely using SSH, you can skip the keyboard entirely, or if you want you can just borrow a keyboard and mouse from another machine for the initial setup before you actually go headless over the network. Raspberry Pi should automatically get an IP address from your router. After your router gives an IP address to your Pi, you can just log in to your router to see the exact IP address that was assigned. You can then connect via SSH using that IP address.

If you don't want to find out what the exact IP address is via the router and instead want to find it out locally, you can pull up the command terminal in Raspbian OS and execute an "ifconfig" command. You can then unplugged your peripherals and go headless from there.

Displays

Moving on to displays, if your TV or monitor has an HDMI input, that's great because all you'll need to get is a cheap HDMI cable. If your monitor only has DVI-in, you'll need an HDMI to DVI cable or an adapter. Just keep in mind that if you do that, the audio signal that's coming out of the HDMI port will be ignored when you're using a DVI converter.

Depending on your setup, you can use external speakers or a splitter. If you're going to go headless, you can skip purchasing a separate monitor specifically for your Pi and just borrow one for the initial setup if you want to. Otherwise, you can still do most of the setup across the network if you are connected via SSH.

Raspberry Pi Casing

Moving forward, even though it may look cool keeping your bare board out with a bunch of wires just hanging off, it is probably not the safest thing to do for your Raspberry Pi. So it is recommended that you get a case for your Pi. You can get a prefab case for as little as $5.00. It is completely optional but it does help protect the board. A number of people have made some pretty cool custom cases, all of which are available for purchase on-line.

Chapter 3: Installing the Operating System In Your SD Card

In this chapter we're going to be looking at operating system options and how to actually install it in your Raspberry Pi. First off, you're going to need to consider what your goal is for your Raspberry Pi. Is this going to be a learning or tinkering board? Are you going to be programming or do you just want a quick and cheap home theater PC? For a more general purpose operating system or for the tinkerer and programmer, most people recommend going for Raspbian OS.

The latest version of Raspbian at the time of this writing is Raspbian Jessie Kernel Version 4.1, which was released in November 2015. For a home theater PC, most people recommend getting either OpenELEC or RaspBMC. If you're just not sure and you want to try multiple operating system versions, get two or three SD cards and you can just install a different operating system on each of them. You can swap them out depending on what you feel like doing with your Raspberry Pi. Below is the link where you can download the various operating systems for your Pi:

https://www.raspberrypi.org/downloads/

The Operating system installation method that we're about to discuss is mainly for those who have a Mac or a Linux desktop. If you have Windows, the concept is still pretty much the same. You'll just use a different program to get the disk image onto your SD card with Windows.

Step 1

Regardless of which type of PC you're using, you're going to need to download the disk image or images of your preferred operating system for your Raspberry Pi. These are by no means the only options, just the ones that the Raspberry Pi community recommends in order to get you started. The first one, as we've mentioned before, is Raspbian.

There's also another version that came out called Occidentalis, which is actually based on Raspbian but has a more educational slant to it and includes a lot more educational tools. For a home theater PC, you'll want to install either OpenELEC or RaspBMC. Both of these are built around the XBMC (Xbox Media Center).

Step 2

Once you have chosen your operating system, click the download link and choose a location in your computer that you're going to easily remember. Once your download is complete, it would probably be in a .zip file format so you'll need to unzip it and you should now have an image file with an .img file extension. There are a lot of different methods to get this image onto the SD card, but if you're on Linux or Mac, we're just going to use the "dd" command to write the image on the card.

We're going with this method mainly because it's installed in almost every UNIX-based system and it should work pretty much the same on all of them. Before we proceed in talking about DD in Mac or Linux, if you're a Windows PC user, you're going to need to download the win32 disc imager. Once you've installed it, you need to run it and tell it where the operating system image file is located on your hard drive and what drive letter to write the image to for your SD card.

When choosing the actual drive letter that points to your SD card, make sure that the SD card you're using is blank since everything inside it is going to be overwritten. Getting back to Linux and Mac, you want to open up a new shell or a terminal as it's called on the Mac, and then navigate to the folder where you downloaded your disk image. In most cases it would be in /Downloads/Raspberry Pi/Raspbian.

Again, keep in mind that you will be overwriting everything on the SD card that you're going to be using for this installation. So use a fresh card or one you don't mind overwriting. At this point, make sure you do not have your SD card reader plugged in yet. The reason for this is because we need to find out which device our SD card will be using.

In your terminal or shell, type "df" (without the quotes) and then press ENTER. Now you should see a list of devices and the folders where they are mounted. This should be any of your internal hard drives or external hard drives and so forth. Now is the time when you want to plug in your SD card into your reader and then plug the reader into an open USB port.

Just wait a few moments for the card to mount. This can take a few seconds. After a few seconds, use the "df" command again. You should now see something different; an item that's listed as either no-name or volume/untitled. On the side you should see something listed like dev/disk3s1 or on Linux it would be something similar to dev/sdb1 or sdc1 or something like that next to it.

Drive assignments may vary from user to user so just take which device is listed next to that volume carefully. You want to make sure that you're using the SD device and not one of your hard drives. DD is an unforgiving command and it will overwrite without prejudice and without asking you if you're sure about doing so. So just be very careful. We can't stress this enough. You don't want to overwrite your main hard drive.

Once you know the device that you're going to write to, remember or write it down. Like what we mentioned earlier, it should be something like dev/disk3s1 on a Mac or something similar to dev/sdc1 on Linux. We're going to change this a little bit since we actually want to write the disk image to the entire card not just a partition on the card, which is what we have mounted right now.

So what we need to do now is unmount the SD card's partition before we can write to the entire card. We don't want to eject the card, we just want to unmount it. On your Mac you can open up your Disk Utility. It's in the same folder as your terminal. You then have to select the volume under the SD card device and click "unmount." You can also do this from the terminal, but you'll need to be on the superuser account. So to use Disk Utility using a superuser or root account, you can type the command below:

```
$ sudo diskutil unmount/dev/disk3s1
```

On Linux you would do a similar thing. You would type in the command below:

```
$ sudo unmount /dev/sdc1
```

You can type the command above or whatever your device assignment happens to be. One thing to remember is that the sudo command will always ask you for the administrator password in order to be able to execute the command, regardless of whether you're using a Mac or a Linux system. Once the SD card's partition is unmounted, we're going to run DD with 3 arguments; "bs," "if," and "of." Those stand for block size, in file, and out file respectively. You'll run the command exactly as below:

```
$ dd bs=1m if=2015-12-24-jessy-raspbian.img of=/dev/sdc1
```

Looking at the command above, you're going to be putting a value for block size; specifically 1m which stands for 1 megabyte, for "if" you'll be putting the name of the image file, and "of" is the location where you stored the image file. Regarding the location of the image file, we're going to change that a little bit. For example, if your device is listed as /dev/disc3s1, you want to change the "of" argument to /dev/rdisk3s1.

This may be different depending on your system so changing this will make sure that you use the entire SD card and not just the partition. In Linux for example, the "of" value would probably be something like /dev/sdb1 or /dev/sdc1. In this case, the letter after the letters "sd" could be different depending on your system. So in order to write to the whole card, you just need to take away the number "1." You should have something similar to the one below:

```
$ dd bs=1m if=2015-12-24-jessy-raspbian.img of=/dev/sdb
```

So that's pretty much of it. Once you're confident that you have the correct arguments for the DD command, hit ENTER. You're going to wait a few minutes while the SD card is being written on. At this point, you won't see any output while this process is ongoing. It will probably take a few minutes so just be patient.

If you're on Linux and you get an error, you might need to change the "bs" value from 1m to 1M (capital M). For some reason the case of the letter matters to a Linux system. Once this has been completed, you should be back to a command prompt. And assuming everything worked properly, you will now have a bootable operating system on your SD card.

You are now ready to boot your Raspberry Pi for the first time and start configuring your system, which we will cover on the next chapter.

Chapter 4: Booting OpenELEC & Raspbian for the First Time On Your Pi

In the last chapter, we installed the operating system on the SD card. Let's now go ahead and insert the SD card into the slot on the underside of the Raspberry Pi. Keep in mind that the metal contacts of the SD card should be facing the underside of the board. First, we'll need at least a keyboard, a mouse, and a monitor. Go ahead and plug the keyboard and mouse to any of the available USB ports. Second, go ahead and plug in the Ethernet CAT5 or CAT6 cable on the Ethernet port on the Pi. Make sure that the other end of the Ethernet cable is plugged into your router. Third, go ahead and plug in the HDMI cable for your monitor.

Do not forget to use an HDMI to DVI converter if you have a DVI monitor. Lastly, plug in the microUSB cable of the 5V power supply to the microUSB port on your Raspberry Pi. Once you have everything plugged in, you should see the LEDs on the board start to light up. You will also see that the boot cycle has now started on the monitor. Just wait for login prompt to appear once the boot process has finished.

Logging In

Once you have the login prompt, you want to use the default username which is "pi", and the default password, which is "raspberry" in all lower case. Once you type those in and press ENTER, you're in.

To start the desktop interface just type "start x" and press ENTER. Most people should be pretty familiar with how this desktop works. It's very similar to most other modern GUI interfaces. Let's now take a look at some of the applications that are available to you once you've successfully started the desktop interface of your Raspberry Pi.

- Scratch – This is basically a programming teaching tool. It is very similar to Karel. If you've ever taken a programming class, they use Karel the robot to teach you basic programming concepts.

- Python – Python is basically a very versatile and robust programming language. It is used by many programmers and companies to make web based applications.

- Midori – Midori is a lightweight web browser. It takes its roots from Mozilla Firefox.

- File Manager – The file manager is very similar to the Window file manager. It lets you see the different directories and storage media that's associated with your Raspberry Pi. It also lets you see the important files in your Raspberry Pi.

- Terminal – Since Raspbian is basically a derivative of Debian Linux, it's no surprise that it also has a terminal similar to Linux. It has the same functions as a Linux terminal. It can also run all the terminal commands that you can run in a Linux system.

Now that we've pretty much seen what the Raspbian operating system looks like, let's go on ahead and see what OpenELEC looks like in a Raspberry Pi. Go ahead and mount the image of OpenELEC onto your SD card. The mounting process for OpenELEC is pretty much the same as Raspbian. If you're still logged into Raspbian on your Raspberry Pi, you must log out and shut the Pi down.

You shut the Raspberry Pi down by using the "halt" command. Again, in order for this command to work, you have to be a superuser. So you need to type in the word "sudo," then put a space by pressing the spacebar, type in the word "halt," and then press ENTER.

After you press ENTER, the Raspberry Pi will initiate the shutdown process. Once finished, you can now switch to the SD card with the OpenELEC operating system. Once the card is inserted, you can start booting your Raspberry Pi with the OpenELEC operating system. As you can see, you can pretty quickly change out cards and be up and running with a different operating system pretty quickly.

Once you have OpenELEC up and running, go ahead and explore the different parts of the operating system, see the different programs it has, and find out what it can do. This is the perfect time to explore and learn what the Raspberry Pi and its operating system is all about.

Chapter 5: How to Get Around in the Raspberry Pi's Unix-based Command Line Interface

In this chapter, we will be going through some of the more basic commands that you're going to need to know in the command line shell for getting around the Unix-based file system. If you're running Raspbian, you'll need to know some of the standard Unix commands. Like most systems in Linux or Unix, files are stored in directory hierarchies.

You can also call them folders if you want to feel more comfortable with that term. When you login, unless you have a custom setting, you will most likely begin in your home/username directory. For Raspbian, the default username that we've been logging in with is Pi. So your home directory is going to be /home/Pi.

Most users on the system, except for root, will have their home directory stored within /home. The main exception is the root user's folder, which is stored in /root. On your command prompt you will see your home directory represented as a tilde symbol "~", and you can use that to easily get back to your home folder anytime.

Moving forward, let's get into working with directories. The first thing you might want to know is where you are and what directory you are located in. The first command that we're going to start with is PWD. PWD stands for Print Working Directory, which tells you the current directory that you're located in at that moment. You'll find that most commands in Unix are abbreviations of the activity that they perform.

As you can see from the output after you typed in PWD and pressed ENTER, you're in /home/pi. If you want to change to another directory, you need to use the CD command. For example, if you want to go to the top level directory—also called the root, which is not to be confused with the root user home directory—you type in this command:

$ cd /

cd / represents the main directory; and the slash that is used is a forward slash. Many people mistakenly use the term backslash when they really mean forward slash. We call the "/" a forward slash because we read from left to right. So a slash leaning to the right is in the forward direction.

Typing the aforementioned command and pressing ENTER will bring you to the top level directory. There is nothing above this top level directory. It only has subdirectories beneath it. With that being said, let's now take a moment to look at a few subdirectories beneath the main root directory.

The first one that we're going to look at is "etc." Etc stores many of the system's configuration files so get familiar with this folder. If you want to change configuration settings, you're going to come here often. To go to the etc subdirectory from the root directory, type in the command below:

$ cd /etc

Now let's take a look at what's inside etc. We do that using the "ls" command. Ls is short for list and it just lists directory contents. ls also have some options associated with it that allows the user to change the way the listing looks.

Let's go ahead and take a look at a few common options of ls:

- -a – lists all files including hidden files in the directory. Files beginning with a dot "." are considered hidden. So anything that you name with a dot preceding the file name will be hidden automatically, unless you use the -a option to list the files.

- -l – lists all the files lengthwise down the screen.

- -p – puts a forward slash after the directory, which is inside the current directory that you are viewing. This lets you easily distinguish directories from files.

- --color – this will give you a colorful directory listing. However, this doesn't always work. This command works depending on the system and if you're logging in remotely.

You can also combine multiple options with a single dash. Look at the example below:

$ ls -lap

Typing the command above will give you all the options that you've indicated together with the list command. Now, to go back a directory, you have two options. In this particular case we can either type cd / to take us back to the main root directory since that's where we started before going into etc, or we can type the command below:

$ cd ..

That's "cd" followed by a space, and then two dots. This takes us back one directory. We also have another command below:

$ cd ../..

This command takes us back two directories if you happen to be two subdirectories in. So if you're still in the "etc" directory, go back one directory. There are a number of other directories to familiarize with within the root directory. Below are some of those directories:

1. /bin – this directory is for commands and binaries.

2. /sbin – this is for system and administrator commands.

3. /user – this is for user-related files. It also has its own /bin and /sbin subdirectories.

4. /var – var stands for variable. The /var/log subdirectory is a common destination for users who troubleshoot problems whose log file end up here.

5. /home – As what we discussed before, this is for the user directories.

6. /mnt – mnt, which stands for Mount, is pretty much the mount point for any external drives, image files, or things like that.

7. /dev – this is for devices that interface with the hardware.

8. /lib – this is for programs and program libraries.

There a lot more, but this is just a quick rundown of the more common directories that you're likely to encounter and use.

So how do we add, remove, or modify files and directories? Well, to create a new directory, type in the command below:

$ mkdir directoryname

Mkdir stands for make directory. This should be followed by a space and then the name of the directory that you want to create. To remove that empty directory, just used the command below:

$ rmdir directoryname

Rmdir stands for remove directory. This should be also followed by a space and then the name of the directory that you want to remove. Keep in mind that using this command with a non-empty directory would result to an error. There's another option to remove a directory even though it contains files and subdirectories. However, it can be a little dangerous in the wrong hands if they don't know what they're doing.

So please use with caution whenever you utilize the below command:

$ rm -rf directoryname

The -r option after the remove command means to do the removing process recursively, which drills down into the subdirectories located within the directory you're trying to remove. The -f option stands for Force, which forces the process to go through. So executing this command basically tells the system that you know what you're doing.

The system will allow you to execute the command as long as you have permission to that file or directory. Again, use these options only if you really need to. There won't be any dialogue box, pop-up window, or anything like that to save you from making a mistake with this command.

For copying files and directories, you'll be using the CP command. Look at the example command below:

$ cp filename1 filename2

First type in the cp command, followed by a space, followed by the name of the file to copy from, followed by another space, and then lastly the name of the file to copy to. Note that filename 1 and filename 2 should be different. Also, keep in mind that you need to have root (sudo) access in order to successfully execute this file.

To rename or move a file without duplicating it, use the command below:

$ mv filename1 filename2

The above command will essentially move the contents of filename1 to filename2. You can also specify directories where files are located. For example, let's say you want to copy the contents of /etc/hosts to your home folder. For that you would use the below command:

$ cp /etc/hosts /home/pi

Type in the cp command, followed by a space, then followed by the file-path of the file that you want to copy, and then another space, and then followed lastly by the file-path of the location where you want to copy the file to.

To move or copy a directory and its subdirectories, you want to use the -r option, which is again a recursive option.

$ cp -r directory1 directory2

If you want to find out about any of these commands, you can use the MAN command. MAN stands for manual. If you want to find out more about the cp command for example, you just have to type the command below:

```
$ man cp
```

This will pull up all the information about the cp command and all the options associated with it. The same applies to the mv, rm, and so forth.

Chapter 6: Python Programming in Raspberry Pi

In this chapter, we're going to look at the best programming language for the Raspberry Pi; Python. It is considered by many as a notably powerful and dynamic language that is used to develop numerous application domains. Most programmers compare Python to Perl, Java, Ruby, Tcl, or Scheme. This is why Python is the primary language the Raspberry Pi is designed to operate on.

Below are some of the key features of the Python programming language:

- Superb for programming veterans and also remain simple enough for beginners to understand.

- Excellent scalability. Python is excellent in small projects; even better for large scale ones.

- Extremely portable and is compatible across all platforms

- Hardware embeddable

- Elegant and simple to understand syntax and semantics

- Excellent stability

- Has a huge standard library of pre-built subroutines, codes, etc.

Moving forward, we'll discuss how to get a very simple python program working. In addition, we'll also discuss how to use the Graphical User Interface to code basic python programs. However, what this chapter won't tackle is the nitty-gritty of learning how to program in Python. Python object-oriented programming is a whole topic in itself and is therefore out of the scope of this book.

Python programming in the Raspberry Pi is similar to Python programming using a normal desktop or laptop computer. It's just that with the Raspberry Pi, you're programming in a very portable, cheap, but robust platform. To start programming with Python on your Raspberry Pi, you must first make sure that you've successfully installed the Raspbian operating system.

Using the desktop of your Raspbian OS, click on the Menu option on the taskbar. Clicking on menu allows you to see the sub-menus for Raspbian. Click on the "Programming" sub-menu. Once you do that, you'll be presented with different programming applications for Raspbian. One of those applications would be your Python Editor.

Python Editors vary depending on the version of Raspbian running in your Raspberry Pi. However, the most common Python IDE would be Stan's Python Editor or SPE. Click on that and you'll be presented with GUI (Graphical User Interface) for your Python IDE (Integrated Development Environment).

The main window of your Python IDE is where you'll type the source code of the program that you're developing. To start making our simple Python program, first create a folder on your Raspbian desktop where we will put our python script. Just right click on any empty space on your desktop and click "Create New Folder." Don't forget to give your new folder a name.

Now, let's go ahead and develop a simple "Hello World" program using Python. To do so, go to the code editor window of your Python IDE and type in the following code:

```
1      print "Hello World"
```

After typing this code in your editor, save it by clicking on the "File" menu at the menu of your Python IDE and then click on "Save." You will have to give your python script a name. In this case, just type in the filename as HelloWorld.py and save it inside the new folder that you have created on your desktop. Take note that filenames should not contain any spaces and that it should have a .py extension. This is the file extension for all Python scripts.

After saving the file, run the program by clicking on the "run" button on the menu bar of your Python IDE. At this point, two things should happen depending on which Python IDE you're using. Some IDEs will pull up the terminal and display the output of the program from there, while other IDEs will have a status bar at the bottom where it will show you the output of the Python program that you just ran.

Regardless of whatever mode of output your IDE uses, it should display the words "Hello World." If you want to run your Python script from the terminal itself and not from the IDE, all you need to do is navigate to where your Python script is located first and run the script from there. To do this, type the command below:

$ cd /home/pi/Desktop/foldername

The "foldername" is the name of the folder that you have created on the desktop. Once you're there type the below command to display the contents of that folder:

$ ls -l

Now, you'll see your HelloWorld.py file. To run this just type in the below command:

$ python HelloWorld.py

The command above is basically telling the system to use the Python interpreter to open the HelloWorld.py file. Press ENTER and you'll see the output; "Hello World."

Congratulations, you've just made your first Python program in your Raspberry Pi.

Chapter 7: Mounting Drives in Raspberry Pi

If you want to plug in an external drive in your Pi, you're going to need to know how to mount it. On most systems like Windows, Mac, and even some Linux systems, when you plug in an external drive, mounting is handled for you automatically. In ejecting or unmounting, however, it is not. That's why we have to safely remove or eject the drive in Windows or Mac. We're going to learn how to do both of those on our Raspberry Pi.

In a Unix system like Linux, a number of devices are set up in the /dev directory to handle things like drives, audio terminals, etc. Since we're only concerned with drives, let's take a look at what is currently mounted on the system. To do that, we use the "df" command. Type the df command in the command prompt similar to what is shown below:

    $ df

Once you type that in and press ENTER, you'll have an output that is closely similar to the one below:

df: `/squashfs': No such file or directory

Filesystem	1K-blocks	Used	Available	Use%	Mounted on
rootfs	7611872	954992	6270220	14%	/
dev	146380	0	146380	0%	/dev
/dev/mmcblkop2	7611872	954992	6270220	14%	/mnt
none	7611872	954992	6270220	14%	/
tmpfs	47708	204	47504	1%	/run
tmpfs	5120	0	5120	0%	/run/lock
tmpfs	95400	0	95400	0%	/run/shm

Looking at the output above, you'll see what is currently mounted on your system. You can see the device names on the left hand side and the directory where they're mounted on the far right. These are also called the mount points.

So let's say that we have a USB thumb drive with some music on it that we want to access, and we want to mount it on the Pi. Before we can plug the drive in, we need to find out what the device name will be. There are two ways to do this. The first is by monitoring your system messages so that when we do plug the drive in, we should see a system message pop up telling us that the device has just become available. You can do that by using the following command:

$ tail -f /var/log/messages

Once you type in the above command and press ENTER, it will display the contents of the messages file as the output. The tail command basically tells the system to look at the tail end of the messages file and keep it open so that if anything is added to it at the bottom, it will display those as well.

Go ahead and plug your thumb drive into any open USB port. If you don't have an open USB port, you will have to either use a hub or just unplug your USB mouse and do without it for now. Once you plug the drive in, you'll see a message pop-up saying that you have a new USB device available and that it is assigned to /dev/sda1. Keep in mind that the drive assignment may vary from system to system, so read the message that pops up carefully to know what your system allocates in your case. For the sake of having an example, we'll just assume that the system assigns your drive to /sda1.

Now that we know that our thumb drive is going to be on /dev/sda1, go ahead and close the messages file by pressing Ctrl+C on your keyboard. There's also another way to find this information out. Just plug your USB drive in and type the command below:

$ sudo fdisk -l

The fdisk command above tells the system to list the connected drives. After you type in the above command and press ENTER, you'll have an output similar to the one below:

Disk /dev/mmcblk0: 7985 MB, 7985954816 bytes

4 heads, 16 sectors/track, 243715 cylinders, total 15597568 sectors

Unites = sectors of 1 * 512 = 512 bytes

Sector size (logical/physical): 512 bytes/ 512 bytes

I/O size (minimum/optimal): 512 bytes / 512 bytes

Disk identifier: 0x00000000

Device Boot	Start	End	Blocks	Id	System
/dev/mmcblk0p1	2048	131071	64512	e	W95 FAT16 (LBA)
/dev/mmcblk0p2	131072	15597567	7733248	83	Linux

Disk /dev/sda: 16.0 GB, 16008609792 bytes

255 heads, 63 sectors/track, 1946 cylinders, total 31266816 sectors

*Units = sectors of 1 * 512 = 512 bytes*

Sector size (logical/physical): 512 bytes / 512 bytes

I/O size (minimum/optimal): 512 bytes / 512 bytes

Disk identifier: 0x00000000

Device Boot	Start	End	Blocks	Id	System
/dev/sda1	32	31266815	15633392	e	W95 FAT32 (LBA)

Looking at the output above, we can see that we now have a device listed at the very bottom and mounted on /dev/sda1. Now that we know where the device is, we need a mount point. There are two places that you could mount this USB drive. One of them is the traditional /mnt directory or you can do /media. Where you mount the drive is totally up to you. Some people prefer /mnt while some prefer /media; it doesn't really matter.

We need to make a mount point in either of these directories. For the sake of making an example, let's go ahead and mount it in /mnt. To do this, go to the /mnt directory by typing in the command below:

```
$ cd /mnt
```

Once you're inside the /mnt directory, go ahead and create a subdirectory called "usbstick" or whatever you want to call it. It's up to you. To make a subdirectory, just type in the command below while you're inside the /mnt directory:

$ sudo mkdir usbstick

A quick and dirty way to get the drive mounted here would be to just mount it as root using the sudo command. Go ahead and type the command below:

$ sudo mount /dev/sda1 /mnt/usbstick

Now, it will mount it there, but the problem with this is that it will only be available to the root user. So we would rather tell the mount command that our regular Pi username can have permission for this drive. We do this by using the command below:

$ sudo mount -t vfat -o uid=pi,gid=pi /dev/sda1 /mnt/usbstick

All right, so let's dissect this command for a moment. First off, we have sudo which tells the system to execute the command as the super user root (and you should be familiar with this already). We then have the mount command which is what we're trying to achieve in this process. Next, you'll notice we've also specified the file system type using the "-t" option. And in the case of a FAT formatted thumb drive, the file system type is "vfat."

Next we have the "-o" which stands for options. Here, we'll tell the mount command to use the user ID Pi along with the group ID Pi for file permissions. In this way, we won't have to use sudo anytime we want to access the drive on our regular Pi user. It will be able to read and write it just fine.

Next in the command is the device name that we learned about earlier by tailing the message log when we plugged the drive in. Lastly is the location to mount the drive. That's the directory that we just created under /mnt called "usbstick." And now, you can access the drive. So let's go ahead and "cd" into that drive by typing the command below:

$ cd /mnt/usbstick

Once you press ENTER after you type in the command above, it'll bring you inside the directory of the drive. Go ahead and see what's inside the drive by typing the command below:

```
$ ls -lap
```

Once you type the command above, press ENTER. You'll see the system list the files that are inside your USB thumb drive. When you're done with the drive, unmounting is even easier. To unmount the drive, you must not be currently accessing it. Thus, you need to get out of the directory of the thumb drive and get out of the mount point location. You do this by typing in the command below:

```
$ cd /mnt
```

Now we can unmount the thumb drive using the "umount" command. Be careful, though, as most beginners make the mistake of typing UNMOUNT instead of UMOUNT. To unmount, type the command below:

```
$ sudo umount /mnt/usbstick
```

You can also unmount using the device name. You do this by using the command below:

```
$ sudo umount /dev/sda1
```

Once you type those umount commands in and press ENTER, you can now safely remove your USB thumb drive. That's it. You can mount hard drives or card readers in pretty much the same way. Just keep in mind that for hard drives, the file system type will probably be different. So for Windows drives, the file system will most likely be NTFS. For Mac drives, it will most likely be HFS+. Thus, remember to use "-t ntfs-3g" for Windows drives and "-t hfsplus" for Mac drives.

Also, keep in mind that hfsplus support is probably not installed by default on the Pi; on Raspbian. So you would need to add a few packages before Mac drives will be able to mount. To do that, you would need to use the command below:

```
$ sudo apt-get install hfsplus hfsutils hfsprogs
```

That way, it will give you support on your Pi for HFS+. There you have it—you're now able to mount drives in your Raspberry Pi.

Chapter 8: Formatting & Partitioning Drives to Connect To Your Pi

So you just bought a new hard drive or thumb drive and you want to partition and format it to work with the Pi. In this chapter, we're going to learn how to do just that. And if you're not familiar with partitioning, partitioning is basically just a way to divide up the drive into smaller pieces. For example, you could turn a 1-Terabyte drive into four 250-Gigabyte partitions. Different operating systems use different partition schemes so you could just use the type that your system wants to see.

For Windows systems, that would be like the master boot record type, or for the Mac, it would be GUID. Linux has its own special type. In this chapter, we're going to take an 8GB hard drive and divide it into two separate 4GB partitions and format them for Linux. There are also command line tools that we will need in order to do this.

The first is called fdisk, which basically allows us to set up partitions on the disk. It's a pretty advanced command and we'll try to make it easier for you to understand. In the preceding chapter, we learned how to find out what drive devices were connected to the system, so let's do that now. Go ahead and type the code below:

```
$ sudo fdisk -l
```

Let's assume that we have an 8GB SD card in a card reader plugged into one of the USB ports. After typing the above command and pressing Enter, you'll have an output similar to the one below:

Disk /dev/mmcblk0: 7985 MB, 7985954816 bytes

4 heads, 16 sectors/track, 243715 cylinders, total 15597568 sectors

Unites = sectors of 1 * 512 = 512 bytes

Sector size (logical/physical): 512 bytes/ 512 bytes

I/O size (minimum/optimal): 512 bytes / 512 bytes

Disk identifier: 0x00000000

Device Boot	Start	End	Blocks	Id	System

/dev/mmcblk0p1	2048	13107164512		e	W95 FAT16 (LBA)
/dev/mmcblk0p2	131072	15597567	7733248	83	Linux

Disk /dev/sda: 7948 MB, 7948206080 bytes

240 heads, 32 sectors/track, 2021 cylinders, total 15523840 sectors

Units = sectors of 1 * 512 = 512 bytes

Sector size (logical/physical): 512 bytes / 512 bytes

I/O size (minimum/optimal): 512 bytes / 512 bytes

Disk identifier: 0x00000000

Device Boot	Start	End	Blocks	Id	System
/dev/sda1	2048	15523839	7760896	b	W95 FAT32

As you can see from the output above, fdisk is telling us that we have our old trusted friend the /dev/sda1 ready to go. Since most hard drives are currently set up for Windows FAT32, let's take a look at how we can change the partitions on this drive to make it a native Linux drive.

For fdisk to work its magic, we need to have root access or be on a super user root account on the system. To do this, we must type in sudo first before fdisk. Go ahead and type the command below:

$ sudo fdisk /dev/sda

In this case, you don't need the number 1 after sda because we're going to work with the main device, not just the first partition. By leaving the number 1 off, we're telling fdisk to work with the whole thing. When we're done, we're going to have an sda1, and we're also going to have an sda2 partition.

Once you type the above command and press ENTER, you'll be met with a different looking command prompt, which says type m for help. Go ahead and type the letter "m" for help and then press ENTER again. Once you do that, you'll have the output below:

Command action

a	*toggle a bootable flag*
b	*edit bsd disklabel*
c	*toggle the dos compatibility flag*
d	*delete a partition*
l	*list known partition types*
m	*print this menu*
n	*add a new partition*
o	*create a new empty DOS partition table*
p	*print the partition table*
q	*quit without saving changes*
s	*create a new empty Sun disklabel*
t	*change a partition's system id*
u	*change display/entry units*
v	*verify the partition table*
w	*write table to disk*
x	*extra functionality*

As you can see, we have a bunch of things we can do here, but we're really only concerned with a handful of them. Let's look at the current partition table on this drive by using the "p" option. Go ahead and type "p" and press ENTER. Once you press p, you'll have the output below:

Disk /dev/sda: 7648 MB, 7948205080 bytes

240 heads, 32 sectors/track, 2021 cylinders, total 15523840 sectors

Units = sectors of 1 * 512 = 512 bytes

Sector size (logical/physical): 512 bytes / 512 bytes

I/O size (minimum/optimal): 512 bytes / 512 bytes

Disk identifier: 0x00000000

Device Boot	Start	End	Blocks	Id	System
/dev/sda1	2048	15523839	7760896	b	W95 FAT32

As you can see, this tells us that we have an 8GB drive with a FAT32 format on it. Let's change that so we can suit it to Linux. What we first want to do is get rid of that Windows partition. Let's use "d" from the Command Action menu list. Type d and press ENTER. As soon as you do that, you'll have an input that says "Selected partition 1." That just deleted the first partition.

Normally it would prompt you if you have more than one drive, but since there's only one partition there, it just went ahead and deleted the first one. Now, let's verify that that happened by using the "p" option again. Go ahead and type p then press ENTER. Once you do that, you'll have the output below:

Disk /dev/sda: 7648 MB, 7948205080 bytes

240 heads, 32 sectors/track, 2021 cylinders, total 15523840 sectors

Units = sectors of 1 * 512 = 512 bytes

Sector size (logical/physical): 512 bytes / 512 bytes

I/O size (minimum/optimal): 512 bytes / 512 bytes

Disk identifier: 0x00000000

Device Boot	Start	End	Blocks	Id	System

Looking at the output, you can see that the drive info for the partition is now gone. Let's now go ahead and create a new Linux partition. We do that by making use of the "n" option from the Command Action menu. Go ahead and type n and then press ENTER. Once you do that, you'll have an output like the one below:

Partition type:

p   *primary (0 primary, 0 extended, 4 free)*

e   *extended*

Right now, the system is basically asking you what type of partition you want to create. In this case, we're creating a primary partition, so go ahead and type in "p" then press ENTER. It would then ask you for a partition number. Just enter the default which is "1" then press ENTER again. After that, it's going to ask you where you want the first sector to be. In this case just use the default, which is 2048.

After entering the default value for the sector, it will then ask you to enter the "Last sector/sectors" value. This is the point where you specify how large you want the partition size to be. You can tell it to utilize everything until the last sector i.e. to use the entire drive, but since we only want two 4GB partitions, we're instead going to tell it how big we want the partition to be.

So we're just going to say 4 Gigabytes here by typing "+4G" and pressing ENTER. After you type +4G and pressed ENTER. Type "p" again to verify that it executed correctly. After typing p and pressing ENTER, you'll have the output below:

Disk /dev/sda: 7648 MB, 7948205080 bytes

240 heads, 32 sectors/track, 2021 cylinders, total 15523840 sectors

Units = sectors of 1 * 512 = 512 bytes

Sector size (logical/physical): 512 bytes / 512 bytes

I/O size (minimum/optimal): 512 bytes / 512 bytes

Disk identifier: 0x00000000

Device Boot	*Start*	*End*	*Blocks*	*Id*	*System*

35

/dev/sda1	2048	8390655	4194304	83	Linux

As you can see, there's now a 4GB Linux partition. Now remember that we want to make two 4GB partitions in our 8GB hard drive. At this point, there's 4GB worth of unpartitioned space left in our hard drive. We'll just do the same process for our second partition with a little variation.

After the output that we saw last, let's type in "n" again from the Command Action menu and press ENTER to make a new partition. It will then ask you again whether you want to make the partition primary or extended. Just go ahead and make it primary like the first partition that we made.

After typing the "p" option to make a primary partition, it will now ask you to enter the partition number. Unlike when we were making our first partition where the default value is 1, this time the default value is 2. Go ahead and type "2" and press ENTER. For the first sector value, you can just use the default sector value here. It's basically using the first sector that's after our first partition.

Since we're not having any more partitions, you can just also use the default value for the last sector. We could use +4G here again. However, depending on how much space we have left, it can either waste space or not make enough. So go ahead and just use the default value for the last sector and press ENTER. Verify by typing p again from the Command Action menu and press ENTER. After pressing ENTER, you'll now have the output below:

Disk /dev/sda: 7648 MB, 7948205080 bytes

240 heads, 32 sectors/track, 2021 cylinders, total 15523840 sectors

Units = sectors of 1 * 512 = 512 bytes

Sector size (logical/physical): 512 bytes / 512 bytes

I/O size (minimum/optimal): 512 bytes / 512 bytes

Disk identifier: 0x00000000

Device Boot	Start	End	Blocks	Id	System
/dev/sda1	2048	8390655	4194304	83	Linux
/dev/sda2	8390656	15523839	3566592	83	Linux

As you can see from the output, we ended up getting less than 4GB for our second partition, but that's okay. Our 8GB drive is really only 7948 MB anyway so we really couldn't technically even make two perfect 4GB partitions for each. Now, we're not done yet as we still have to write this information into the partition table. Our FAT32 partition is technically actually still there and no changes have yet been made to the drive. So you can actually quit this if you wanted to and roll back to the FAT32 partition.

The process that we just executed is just telling fdisk what we want to do. Now, we have to tell fdisk that we're ready to do it and we want to write it to the drive. To do that, we have to make use of the "w" option from the Command Action menu. Go ahead and type w and press ENTER. After you press ENTER, you'll have the output below:

The partition table has been altered!

Calling ioctl() to re-read partition table.

Syncing disks.

$

After you get the above output, go ahead and verify that everything that we did was applied to the drive by typing the command below:

$ sudo fdisk -l

Press ENTER after you've entered the command above. You'll have the output below:

Disk /dev/mmcblk0: 7985 MB, 7985954816 bytes

4 heads, 16 sectors/track, 243715 cylinders, total 15597568 sectors

Unites = sectors of 1 * 512 = 512 bytes

Sector size (logical/physical): 512 bytes/ 512 bytes

I/O size (minimum/optimal): 512 bytes / 512 bytes

Disk identifier: 0x00000000

Device Boot	Start	End	Blocks	Id	System
/dev/mmcblk0p1	2048	13107164512	e	W95 FAT16 (LBA)	
/dev/mmcblk0p2	131072	15597567	7733248	83	Linux

Disk /dev/sda: 7948 MB, 7948206080 bytes

240 heads, 32 sectors/track, 2021 cylinders, total 15523840 sectors

Units = sectors of 1 * 512 = 512 bytes

Sector size (logical/physical): 512 bytes / 512 bytes

I/O size (minimum/optimal): 512 bytes / 512 bytes

Disk identifier: 0x00000000

Device Boot	Start	End	Blocks	Id	System
/dev/sda1	2048	8390655	4194304	83	Linux
/dev/sda2	8390656	15523839	3566592	83	Linux

We now have two partitions: sda1 and sda2. Now, we need to format them before we can mount them to the system and use them to store data. In Linux, the native file system you probably want to use is ext4. There are many other file systems in Linux and they all have their pros and cons. For now, though, just stick with ext4.

The next tool or command that you're going to want to use is mkfs, which is short for make file system. As usual, we need to be a super user/root to use it. Go ahead and type in the following command:

$ sudo mkfs -t ext4 /dev/sda1

As you can see in the command above, we've specified that we want to use the ext4 file system on the sda1 partition. After you've pressed ENTER, you'll have an output that is closely similar to the one below:

mke2fs 1.42.5 (dd-mm-yyyy)

Filesytem label=

OS type: Linux

Block size=4096 (log=2)

Fragment size=4096 (log=2)

Stride=0 blocks, Stripe width=0 blocks

262144 inodes, 1048576 blocks

52428 blocks (5.00%) reserved for the super user

First data block=0

Maximum filesystem blocks=1073741824

32 block groups

32768 blocks per group, 32768 fragments per group

8192 inodes per group

Superblock backups stored on blocks:

3276, 98304, 163840, 229376, 294912, 819200, 884736

Allocating group tables: done

Writing inode tables: done

Creating journal (32768 blocks): done

Writing superblocks and filesystem accounting information: done

Once that is done, you will have a formatted file system that is native to Linux with ext4. Now, you want to do the same thing with the second partition, but instead of using sda1, you should use sda2. Do that by typing the command below and then pressing ENTER:

$ sudo mkfs -t ext4 /dev/sda2

Now you have both of these partitions and they are ready to be mounted. We will need two directories to mount them in so let's go to our /mnt directory by typing "cd /mnt" on our command prompt. Once you're there, just make two directories by using the mkdir command. You can name the two directories whatever you like, but for our example, we'll just name them part1 and part2. Go ahead and type the command below while in the /mnt directory:

$ sudo mkdir part1 part2

As you can see from the command above, we're making two directories with one command. So let's go ahead and mount sda1 to part1 and sda2 to part2. Right now, we're going to mount these partitions using root permission. However, if you want your regular Pi user to be able to use this drive, you should use the "-o" option and then specify the group ID and the user ID. To do this, you must enter the command below:

$ sudo mount -o gid=pi,uid=pi /dev/sda1 /mnt/part1

As you can see, we've entered -o gid=pi,uid=pi in between the mount command and the device path. So let's mount our first partition. As was mentioned earlier, we're going to use root permission to mount by using the command below:

$ sudo mount /dev/sda1 /mnt/part1

Using the above command will mount the first partition into that folder or directory that we just created called part1. Let's now do the same for the second partition by typing in the command below:

$ sudo mount /dev/sda2 /mnt/part2

After entering those two commands for both partitions, let's try it out. Let's go ahead and "cd" into part1 by typing the command below:

$ cd part1

Let's now see if we can write data in this partition by creating a file. Type in the command below:

$ sudo touch test1

Verify if the file was successfully created in the directory by listing the files using the command below:

$ ls -la

Once you've typed that command in and press ENTER, you'll have an output like the one below:

drwxr-xr-x 3   *root   root   4096 MM DD hh:mm .*

drwxr-xr-x 5   *root   root   4096 MM DD hh:mm ..*

drwx------- 2   *root   root   16384 MM DD hh:mm lost+found*

-rw-r--r-- 1   *root   root   0   MM DD hh:mm test1*

As you can see from the output, we now have a file named "test1" in the directory. Let's now do the same for the second partition. So from the part1 directory, just type in the command below:

$ cd ../part2

It'll immediately bring you to the part2 directory that you've created. Create a file to verify that we can store data on this partition by entering the command below:

$ sudo touch test2

Again, verify if the file was successfully created in the directory by listing the files using the command below:

$ ls -la

Once you've typed that command in and press ENTER, you'll have an output like the one below:

drwxr-xr-x	*3*	*root*	*root*	*4096*	*MM DD hh:mm*	*.*
drwxr-xr-x	*5*	*root*	*root*	*4096*	*MM DD hh:mm*	*..*
drwx-------	*2*	*root*	*root*	*16384*	*MM DD hh:mm*	*lost+found*
-rw-r--r--	*1*	*root*	*root*	*0*	*MM DD hh:mm*	*test2*

As you can see from the output, we have successfully created a test2 file in the directory.

So that's basically it. We've just created two Linux partitions and mounted them. When you're done with these new drives and you want to take them out of the USB port, don't forget to unmount them by using the command below:

$ sudo umount /dev/sda1

$ sudo umount /dev/sda2

Raspberry (2nd Edition) : Raspberry Pi2 Programming Made Easy

Chapter 9: Raspberry Pi Networking – Setting Up a Static IP & Wifi

In this chapter, we'll talk about how to configure a static IP address so that if you wanted to host your Pi at home or even at a paid collocation hosting facility, you could do so. We'll also talk about how to set up your Pi to work on WiFi using a tiny USB WiFi adapter. But first, let's get started by setting up a static IP address on our wired connection to the router.

Up to this point, if you've been connecting your Pi to your router and have been using it online already, your IP address was assigned via DHCP or the dynamic host configuration protocol. Your router uses this protocol to assign each device on your network its own IP address. No two devices on your local network can have the same IP address.

What we want to do is tell our Pi to use a specific IP address that will not change each time we started up our Raspberry Pi. It's important to have a static IP rather than a randomly assigned dynamic IP. This is because if we want to use the Pi as a server, we could configure the router to forward incoming server reports to our Pi and allow connections from the Internet into our local network to connect to the Pi.

By having this capability, you could serve web pages and files or you could even use it as an on-the-go music server if you wanted to. So let's take a look at the file that we need to edit to update the configuration changes so that we can have a static IP. First, go to the network directory by typing in the command below:

$ cd /etc/network

Once you're in the network directory, list the contents of the directory by typing the command below:

$ ls

What we want to do next after we list the files that are inside the network directory is to edit the "interfaces" file. Before we do that, though, let's take a look at the IP address that we are currently using. To do this, type in the command below:

$ ifconfig

Once your press ENTER after typing the "ifconfig" command, you'll most likely have an output similar to the one below:

eth0   Link encap:Ethernet   Hwaddr b8:27:eb:e5:cf:9a

inet addr:192.168.0.210   Bcast:0.0.0.0   Mask:255.255.255.0

UP BROADCAST RUNNING MULTICAST MTU:1500 Metric:1

RX packets:390 errors:0 dropped:0 overruns:0 frame:0

TX packets:320 errors:0 dropped:0 overruns:0 carrier:0

collisions:0 txqueuelen:1000

RX bytes:30902 (30.1 KiB)   TX bytes:51715 (50.5 KiB)

lo   Link encap:Local Loopback

inet addr:127.0.0.1 Mask:255.0.0.0

UP LOOPBACK RUNNING MTU:16436 Metric:1

RX packets:0 errors:0 dropped:0 overruns:0 frame:0

TX packets:0 errors:0 dropped:0 overruns:0 carrier:0

collisions:0 txqueuelen:0

RX bytes:0 (0.0 B) TX bytes:0 (0.0B)

As you can see on interface "eth0," we have an IP address of 192.168.0.210. Keep in mind that the IP address that we have here is for example purposes only. The actual IP address that you will have on your device would be different.

Going back to our example, note that anything beginning with 192.168 is what is called a non-routable IP address. This was an address space that was set aside for local networks only. No public machine on the Internet can have an address beginning with those numbers.

There are also some routers that use an IP range within 10.10 instead of 192.168 to assign an IP address to a device within a local network. What your router does in order to get your local devices connected to the Internet is what's called a NAT or network address translation. In a NAT, your Internet provider gives you one IP address that is assigned to your modem/router. That address is usually dynamic, meaning it can change from time to time or pretty much anytime you disconnect and reconnect your modem.

It basically depends on your provider how often your router's IP address will change. So what happens is your router handles requests from each of your local devices. It then sends those requests out to the Internet on its public IP address that was assigned by your ISP. When the response comes back from across the Internet from whatever server you connected to, the router knows how to send that response back to the correct device on your local network.

As far as anyone on the Internet is concerned, you only really have one IP address even though you may have a hundred devices behind your local network that have non-routable IP addresses locally.

Now that we have that out of the way, let's make our IP address static on our Raspberry Pi. Let's just assume that our device has an IP address of 192.168.0.210 as indicated in our example output after typing in the "ifconfig" command. Since our Pi currently has that IP address designation and we know that no other devices on our network are using that address, let's make that IP address static for our Pi.

Open the "interfaces" file in the /etc/network directory by typing in the command below:

$ sudo pico interfaces

Once you type that in and press ENTER, you'll see what's written in the interfaces file. You'll probably have an output similar to the one below:

auto lo

iface lo inet loopback

iface etho inet dhcp

Since we now have access to the content of the interfaces file using root access, we can now make changes to it. As you can see from our output above, we have the line:

iface etho inet dhcp

What we want to do now is change the "dhcp" into "static." Once you've made the changes, you should how have something that looks like the one below:

auto lo

iface lo inet loopback

iface etho inet static

Once that's done, we need to define what IP address we want as well as some other network options. So go down a line from "iface etho inet static," press TAB, and type in the following entries:

address 192.168.0.210

netmask 255.255.255.0

network 192.168.0.0

broadcast 192.168.0.255

gateway 192.168.0.1

Once you finish typing the entries, your interfaces file should now look like the one below:

auto lo

iface lo inet loopback

iface eth0 inet static

address 192.168.0.210

netmask 255.255.255.0

network 192.168.0.0

broadcast 192.168.0.255

gateway 192.168.0.1

Take note that the gateway IP address may be different for you because this is going to be the local IP address of your router. It will probably be different from our example. Usually routers have a default of either 192.168.1.1 or 192.168.0.1. Basically, whatever IP address you use when you configured your router, just use that. Once you've type everything in, save your changes to the interfaces file by pressing Ctrl+O and then exit the text editor by pressing Ctrl+X.

At this point, it is recommended that you reboot your Pi. There is a way to simply reload the networking interfaces to implement the changes, but just to be on the safe side, you should instead reboot the system by typing in the command below:

$ sudo reboot

If you're connected locally to the Pi's own keyboard and monitor, you could just bring the network interface back up and down to implement the changes by typing in the command below:

$ sudo ifconfig eth0 down

$ sudo ifconfig eth0 up

If you did that and everything is fine, then great. But if you rebooted, once the Pi is back up, you should be able to log in from any machine on your network using the static IP address that you chose. So for example, on the Mac, you can go to the terminal and use SSH to do a remote login. On the Mac terminal, type in the following command:

ssh -l pi 192.168.0.210

After typing that in, it'll then ask you for the Pi username's password. Just type in the password and press ENTER. And there you go—you're not logged in remotely to your Raspberry Pi. That basically says that we opened a secure shell with the login name Pi at the address 192.168.0.210.

For Windows, you can also use a program called Putty to remotely log in to your Raspberry Pi using the static IP. That's basically all there is to it. Your Pi will not always have the same IP address so that if you wanted to provide a route into it from your router for either web traffic or remote, you'd be able to do so.

Before we get into configuring WiFi for the Raspberry Pi, let's talk about DNS servers for a moment. If you wanted to define your DNS servers, you can do that as well. For those who don't know, DNS servers are basically the Yellow Pages of the Internet. It contains the IP addresses of all the servers in the Internet.

When you type something like, say, Google.com in your browser, your DNS server goes and looks that up and will tell you that Google.com is located at IP address 74.125.224.167. And since it would be impossible to remember every address that has just a number scheme like that on the Internet, DNS is basically like your Internet Phone book and it looks those addresses up for you.

Let's look at the DNS settings for our Raspberry Pi. First, go to the /etc directory of your Pi and then open up the "resolv.conf" file by typing in the command below:

```
$ cd /etc
$ sudo pico resolv.conf
```

Once you type those in, you'll now see the content of the resolv.conf, which is similar to the one line of code below:

nameserver 192.168.0.1

As you can see, we only have the nameserver and our example router's IP address. What this means is that we just have our router serving up DNS requests which it then forwards on to the Internet Service Provider's DNS servers. If you wanted to use some other type of nameserver like Google's DNS servers or OpenDNS, you could specify those here in the resolv.conf file. To do that, simply delete your router's IP address and replace it with the IP of the DNS of your choice.

For example, if you want to use Google's DNS servers, you would have to modify your "resolv.conf" file to look like the one below:

nameserver 8.8.8.8

nameserver 8.8.4.4

You might be wondering why we made two entries. Google's DNS has a secondary server so if you want, you can use only one or both. If in case you encounter any outbound connection troubles on the Internet, you may need to set up your default gateway. So you do that like this:

```
$ sudo route add default gw 192.168.0.1 eth0
```

As what was mentioned before, you want to use your router's local IP address here. Don't use 192.168.0.1 like our example unless your router also happens to have the exact same IP address. Now, let's take a look at our routing information by typing the command "route" on your command prompt and pressing ENTER.

Once you press ENTER, you'll have the output below:

Kernel IP routing table

Destination	Gateway	Genmask	Flags	Metric	Ref	Use	Iface
default	myrouter	0.0.0.0	UG	0	0	0	eth0
192.168.0.0	*	255.255.255.0	U	0	0	0	eth0

Now you can see that we've set our default route—our default gateway—to our router which is 192.168.0.1. If you want to give your Pi a hostname, you can set that in the hostname file. The hostname file is also located in the same directory of our interfaces file i.e. in /etc/network.

Let's now access the hostname file by typing in the command below while in the /etc/network directory:

```
$ sudo pico hostname
```

You'll most likely see a single line of text which is your current hostname in there. Just change it to whatever hostname you want your Pi to have and save it.

Now, let's set up WiFi for our Raspberry Pi. To give your Raspberry Pi wireless capability, you have to use USB WiFi adapter. You can purchase a USB WiFi adapter from any computer store near your area. To set the USB WiFi adapter, let's first go to our /etc/network directory again.

```
$ cd /etc/network
```

We'll be editing the interfaces file again here so enter the command below:

$ sudo pico interfaces

Once there, we're going to look over the wlano section. If you don't have one, you need to create it. However, chances are high that you have one. So if you want use DHCP to set up your IP address automatically for the WiFi connection, you must have the following entries in your interfaces file:

allow-hotplug wlano

auto wlano

iface wlano inet dhcp

wpa-ssid "YOURSSID"

wpa-psk "YOURWIFIPASSWORD"

Take note that "YOUSSID" here refers to your Wifi name, i.e. the name of the connection when you detect the WiFi signal, while "YOURWIFIPASSWORD" refers to the password that you use to connect to your WiFi. Once you type those in, you're interfaces file should now look like this:

auto lo

iface lo inet loopback

iface etho inet static

address 192.168.0.210

netmask 255.255.255.0

network 192.168.0.0

broadcast 192.168.0.255

gateway 192.168.0.1

allow-hotplug wlano

auto wlano

iface wlano inet dhcp

    wpa-ssid "YOURSSID"

    wpa-psk "YOURWIFIPASSWORD"

Note that in your interfaces file, you have the settings for both your wired and wireless connections indicated. Once you save that and reboot, you should automatically get a wireless IP address. If you also want a static IP address for your wireless connection, here's how you set that up.

To use a static IP for your WiFi connection, type in the changes to your interfaces file similar to the one below:

auto lo

iface lo inet loopback

iface etho inet static

address 192.168.0.210

netmask 255.255.255.0

network 192.168.0.0

broadcast 192.168.0.255

gateway 192.168.0.1

allow-hotplug wlano

auto wlano

iface wlano inet static

    address 192.168.0.211

    netmask 255.255.255.0

network 192.168.0.0

broadcast 192.168.0.255

gateway 192.168.0.1

wpa-ssid "YOURSSID"

wpa-psk "YOURWIFIPASSWORD"

Keep in mind that the SSID and WiFi password are both case-sensitive so make sure you have all the cases typed in correctly and in between quotes. As you can see from our example above, we have both the wired and wireless connections for our Raspberry Pi on static IPs. Save the file and reboot your Raspberry Pi to implement the changes.

Conclusion

Thank you for purchasing and reading this book. We hope that we've taught you all the basic things that you need to know about your Raspberry Pi; how to set it up, how to install the operating system so that you'll be able to develop programs using it.

From here, developing more intricate programs using Python is just a matter of learning the nitty-gritty of the programming language itself. There are many online tutorials out there that you can go and see to get in-depth knowledge of Python programming. Python is a very versatile and stable programming language and using it to make your Pi do wondrous things is easy, as long as you have an advanced knowledge of the programming language itself.

Again, Thank you so much and we hope that you succeed in your quest for knowledge on the Python programming language and that you have fun in finding ingenious ways to use your Raspberry Pi.